MR. BEAN'S HOLIDAY

Joke Book for Kids

CARLTON
BOOKS

This edition first published by Carlton Books Ltd 2007
20 Mortimer Street
London
WIT 3JW

First published as 'The Mr Bean Joke Book' by Carlton Books
Ltd in 2002
Text and design Copyright ° 2002 Carlton Books Ltd

TM & ° Tiger Aspect Productions Ltd 2007
www.mrbean.com

A CIP catalogue for this book is available from the British
Library.

ISBN 978-1-84442-398-9

Text by Rod Green
Editorial Manager Rod Green
Designer Michelle Pickering
Production Janette Burgin

CONTENTS

MonDay Jokes

Squirt!

Monday is a funny old day. It's a sad day and a happy day both at the same time. It's a sad day because the weekend is over. **BOO!** But it's a happy day because it's the start of a whole brand spanking new week. **HOORAH!**

Monday is back to school day. **BOO!** But not for me. **HOORAH!**

And not on Bank Holidays, half term, summer holidays and Christmas holidays! **DOUBLE HOORAH!**

Monday is also the day I like to go to the library. **HOORAH!**

Sshhh!! No cheering in the library. So, if your Monday is a happy day, then here are some jokes to make you even happier. If your Monday is a sad day, then read these jokes and

FOR GOODNESS SAKE CHEER UP!!

WHY SHOULD YOU NEVER GO INTO THE JUNGLE ON A MONDAY AT LUNCHTIME?

That's when the elephants have their parachute practice.

Why do ducks have **flat** feet?

They went into the jungle on a Monday at lunchtime.

Ha Ha Ha

The teacher was giving a lesson on the ancient Romans and suspected that a boy near the back of the class hadn't been paying attention.

'**Colin,**' said the teacher, '**can you tell me what a forum is?**'

'**Er ...**' mumbled Colin, '**a two-um plus two-um, Miss?**'

$$2+2$$

* * * * * *

What do you call a cow with two legs?

Lean beef.

What do you call a cow with no legs?

Ground beef.

What's the difference between a teacher who drones on and on and on and on and on and on ... and a bad book?

You can shut the book up.

WHAT GOES BLACK-WHITE-BLACK-WHITE-BLACK-WHITE?

A PENGUIN ROLLING DOWN AN ICEBERG.

What happens to **witches** who get into trouble at magic school?

THEY'RE EX-SPELLED.

What's black and white and awkward?

A MATHS TEST.

£££ One Monday morning a man went for a job interview and was told there and then that he'd got the job.

'You'll get **£15,000** to start with,' said his boss,' 'and **£20,000** after six months.'

'Great,' said the man. 'i'll be back in six months.'

WHAT WAS THE BOOKWORM
DOING IN THE LIBRARY?
TRYING TO BURROW A BOOK.

❧ ❧ ❧ ❧ ❧ ❧ ❧ ❧ ❧ ❧ ❧ ❧

The headmaster addressed the pupils at the school assembly one morning.

'I have some GOOD NEWS and some BAD NEWS,' **he said.** 'The good news is that we are only having half a day at school this morning ...'

There was wild cheering and applause.

' ... the bad news is that we're having the other half this afternoon.'

❧ ❧ ❧ ❧ ❧ ❧ ❧ ❧ ❧ ❧ ❧ ❧

WHAT'S THE COMPLAINING TEACHER'S FAVOURITE DAY?
MOANDAY.

A man made an appointment to see his bank manager on a Monday morning.

'**What can I do for you today?**' asked the bank manager.

'**I'd like you to check my balance**,' said the man.

'**Certainly**,' said the bank manager. '**Can you stand on one leg on this beach ball?**'

A new boy started at school and was settling in to his first class. **'WHAT'S YOUR NAME?'** asked the teacher.

'Fred Frederick Frederico Frederooni Frederango Mickey Frederickson Smith,' the boy replied.

'WELL,' smiled the teacher, **'WE'LL JUST CALL YOU FRED SMITH, SHALL WE?'**

'Oh, my dad won't like that,' said the boy.

'WHY NOT?' asked the teacher.

'He doesn't like people taking the Mickey out of my name.'

Why couldn't the music
teacher open the piano?

ALL THE KEYS WERE INSIDE.

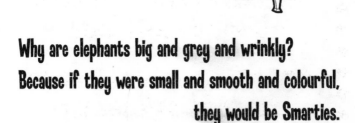

Why are elephants big and grey and wrinkly?
Because if they were small and smooth and colourful,
they would be Smarties.

The history teacher was teaching
the class about the Kings and
Queens of England.
'Who followed Edward VI?' he asked.
'Mary,' said a girl near the
front.
'And who followed Mary?'
'Her little lamb?'

A policeman was walking along the street when he saw a little girl on her way to school. She was desperately stretching to reach a door knocker. Always willing to help, the policeman walked over to her.

'**i can do that for you**,' he said, and loudly rapped the knocker three times.

'**BRILLIANT!**' said the little girl. '**NOW RUN LIKE MAD!**'

What goes, 'Pant ... pant ...'?

A PAIR OF PANTS.

Why could people never find the purple book in the library?

It was often taken to be red.

What do you call the small streams that run into the River Nile?

THE JUVENILES.

What do you call a sheep with no legs?
A CLOUD.

The teacher had noticed that one of her pupils
hadn't been at school the previous day.
'Claire,' she said, 'you missed school
yesterday, didn't you?'
'Yes, Miss,' said Claire, 'but not very much.'

Two bags of chips went into a pub on a Monday at lunchtime and each ordered a pint of lager.

'Sorry,' **said the barman,** 'I'm afraid we don't serve food.'

What's green and hard?
A frog with a flick knife.

What's black and white and hard?
A MATHS TEST.

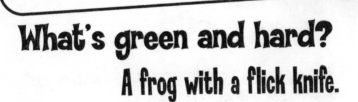

What's big and fat and hums?
An opera singer who can't
remember the words.

❦ ❦ ❦ ❦ ❦ ❦ ❦ ❦ ❦ ❦ ❦

Kevin's father was called in to the
school to see the Headmaster.
'What's the problem?' asked
Kevin's dad. 'Has Kevin done
something wrong?'
'He certainly has,' said the
Headmaster. 'He peed in the
school swimming pool.'
'Oh, come, now,' said Kevin's dad.
'That's not so bad, is it? Lots of
kids pee in swimming pools.'
'Not from the top diving board
they don't!'

APRIL 1ST

Why is everybody so tired on April 1st?
Because we've just had a long 31-day March.

A little boy arrived home from school.

'HOW DID YOU GET ON AT SCHOOL TODAY?'
asked his mother.

'THE TEACHER WAS A BIT ANGRY WITH ME,'
said the boy, 'BECAUSE I COULDN'T
REMEMBER WHERE THE PENINES WERE.'

'WELL NEXT TIME BE
MORE CAREFUL WHERE
YOU PUT THINGS!'

Two monsters were on their way to school.

'We had burglars last night,' said the first one.

'Oooh!' said his pal. **'We've never had burglars. What was it like?'**

'Not bad,' said the first monster. **'But they don't taste as nice as teachers.'**

A MAN had an appointment to see the bank manager at the bank on a Monday morning. He walked into the man's office and found him sitting in a small tree. It turned out he was the branch manager.

'I don't want to go to school today, Mummy! The teachers all think I'm an idiot and the kids all hate me!'

'But you have to go, darling. You're the HEADMASTER.'

Two boys were on their way to school on a Monday morning.

'I hate maths,' said one. **'I'd do anything to get out of maths. I'm thinking about setting the maths teacher's trousers on fire today again.'**

'What do you mean again?' said the other.

'Well, I thought about it last Monday as well.'

'SMITH!' YELLED THE ENGLISH TEACHER AS HE ENTERED THE CLASSROOM. 'PASS THESE BOOKS ROUND TO THE REST OF THE CLASS. JONES, CLEAN THE BLACKBOARD. BROWN, COLLECT LAST NIGHTS' HOMEWORK FROM EVERYONE. AND YOU, NEW BOY, WHAT IS YOUR NAME?'

'KEVIN, SIR,' ANSWERED THE BOY.

'WE DON'T USE FIRST NAMES IN MY CLASS, BOY. WHAT'S YOUR LAST NAME?'

'DARLING,' REPLIED THE BOY. 'KEVIN DARLING.'

'VERY WELL, KEVIN, WELCOME TO THE CLASS ...'

WHY WAS THE CROSS-EYED TEACHER SACKED?
She couldn't control her pupils.

An exchange student in an English school was having real problems with how to pronouce English words correctly. Words like 'THOUGHT', 'ENOUGH', 'BOUGHT', 'BOUGH' and 'THOUGH' were giving him real problems because they just weren't pronounced anything like their spellings.

He eventually gave up and went home when he saw a local newspaper headline which read;

The Daily Blah

SHOW PRONOUNCED SUCCESS

What's showerproof, wears a mask and rides through the desert?
The Lone Raincoat.

What's the difference between a
fisherman and a bored librarian.
**One baits his hooks, the other
hates his books.**

'I'M REALLY GLAD YOU DECIDED TO CALL
ME JAMES,' said a little boy to his mother as
she picked him up from school one day.
'WHY'S THAT?' asked his mum.
'BECAUSE THAT'S WHAT EVERYONE AT
SCHOOL CALLS ME, TOO.'

How do you make a **WITCH** squirm?
Give the witch '**T**' to make her **TWITCH**.

How do you make a **WITCH** scratch?
Drop the '**W**' to make her **ITCH**.

A librarian was fast asleep at home in the middle of the night when the phone rang. 'WHAT TIME DOES THE LIBRARY OPEN?' asked the caller.

'NINE O'CLOCK,' said the librarian, 'BUT WHY ARE YOU CALLING ME NOW? SURELY YOU COULD WAIT UNTIL NINE O'CLOCK TO GET INTO THE LIBRARY.'

'I DON'T WANT TO GET IN.' said the caller. 'I WANT TO GET OUT.'

THE LOCAL LIBRARIAN STUCK HER HEAD IN A HAMBURGER. SOMEONE SAID HER HAIR WOULD LOOK NICE IN A BUN.

A frog went into the job centre and asked the man behind the desk if he could find him a job.

'A talking frog?' said the man in amazement. 'Of course I can.'

The man made one phone call and handed the frog a piece of paper.

'There you go,' he said, 'you start rehearsals for your own TV show on Monday.'

'But that's no good to me,' said the frog. 'I'm a plumber.'

What did they call the girl at school who kept an encyclopedia in her knickers?

SMARTY PANTS.

THE SCHOOL PUT ON A MUSICAL TO RAISE FUNDS FOR ESSENTIAL REPAIRS AND JOHNNY GOT THE STAR PART. ALL THE PARENTS CAME TO WATCH, BUT AS JOHNNY STEPPED FORWARD TO SING HIS BIG NUMBER, HE FELL STRAIGHT THROUGH SOME ROTTEN BOARDS.

'DON'T WORRY,' HIS FATHER WHISPERED TO HIS MOTHER. 'IT'S JUST A STAGE HE'S GOING THROUGH.'

When his father saw his school report, he asked his son why he always did so badly at arithmetic.

'Well,' said the little boy, 'I reckon there are three kinds of people in the world. Those who can count, and those who can't.'

It was first thing in the afternoon and the teacher stood in front of her class. They'd had a biology lesson about insects that morning and now it was English, so the teacher decided to try to maintain the theme

'All right, class,' she said. 'Who can give me a sentence using the word ANTENNAE?'

'I CAN,' said little Claire. 'WE ALL WANTED CHIPS FOR LUNCH BUT THERE ANTENNAE.'

What do you get if you cross a carpet with an elephant?
A deep pile in your living room.

TueSday JOKES

Yum! Yum!

Tuesday is a bit of a **DULL DAY**. If Tuesday had a colour it would be a blue day. **TEDDY** likes Tuesday because it's the day that I make any minor repairs to him. He does seem to be quite accident prone. Tuesday is also the day I give the **GOLDFISH** new water, even though he never finishes drinking the last lot. **SCRAPPER** likes to hang around when I'm doing that, just in case the goldfish gets loose and he can snap him up. He never does, though ... except for that one time ... It took me ages to get that stupid cat to spit out the fish. Teddy and the goldfish and me often laugh about that now. Well, I do anyway, but not as much as you'll laugh at these Tuesday jokes. Most of my Tuesdays seem to be taken up with animals one way or another, so most of these Tuesday jokes are about animals, too. There's no point in trying to tell jokes to animals, though. The only ones that ever laugh are hyenas! **HA-HA!**

What's the best thing for a sick bird?
TWEETMENT.

Where do baby apes sleep?
In apricots.

What has a bad smell and flies?
A dead skunk.

WHY WON'T LITTLE CRABS LET ANY OF THE OTHER SEA CREATURES PLAY WITH THEIR TOYS?
THEY'RE SHELLFISH.

How do you stop fish from smelling?
Put clothes pegs on their noses.

TWO fish were in a tank.
ONE turned to the
other and said, 'CAN YOU
DRIVE THIS THING?'

What did Tarzan say when
he saw the elephants
coming on a Tuesday?
'Here come the elephants.'

What did Tarzan say when
he saw the elephants
coming on a Tuesday
wearing sunglasses?
Nothing. He didn't
recognise them.

A man went into a pet shop one Tuesday morning to buy a new pet and the shop assistant offered him a mouse.

'This is no ordinary mouse,' said the shop assistant. 'He can talk.'
'Rubbish!' said the man. 'Mice can't talk!'

'OH. I CAN. SIR.' said the mouse, 'AND I REALLY NEED A NEW HOME. I'VE HAD SIX OWNERS IN THE PAST THREE WEEKS BUT NONE OF THEM UNDERSTOOD HOW SPECIAL I AM. I CAN RUN A MILE FASTER THAN A FERRARI.

I CAN COOK BETTER THAN JAMIE OLIVER AND ONCE HAD A TRIAL AS GOAL KEEPER FOR MANCHESTER UNITED. I SWAM THE ENGLISH CHANNEL A MONTH AGO, I CAN SING OPERA, PLAY THE PIANO AND I KNOW HOW TO PROGRAMME A VIDEO RECORDER PROPERLY.'

'This mouse is incredible!' **said the man.** 'How come he's had six owners in the past three weeks?'

'Unfortunately,' **said the shop assistant,** 'they just couldn't put up with his constant lies.'

squeak!

How do you get down from a camel?
YOU DON'T. YOU GET DOWN FROM A DUCK.

• • • • • • • • • • • • •

What do you call a camel with three humps **?**

HUMPHREY.

• • • • • • • • • • • • • • • • • • •

WHAT DO YOU GET IF YOU CROSS A GIRAFFE WITH A PORCUPINE**?**

A walking toilet brush.

• • • • • • • • • • • • • • • •

WHAT DO YOU GET A REALLY GRUMPY TIGER FOR HIS BIRTHDAY?

I don't know, but you'd better hope he likes **IT!**

Scrapper once drank a whole pint of milk from his bowl in less than six seconds. **IT WAS A LAP RECORD.**

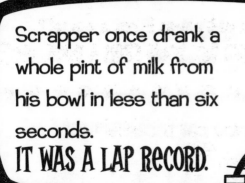

What do you call a lion without an eye?
A LON.

• • • • • • • • • • • • • • • • • • • •

Why are eagles cleverer than chickens?
Ever heard of Kentucky Fried Eagle?

• • • • • • • • • • • • • • • • • • • •

WHY COULDN'T THE TWO ELEPHANTS GO SWIMMING ON TUESDAY?
THEY ONLY HAD ONE PAIR OF TRUNKS.

HOW do you make a **CAT** float?

You drop some ice cream into a glass of coke and add one freshly squeezed cat.

✢ ✢ ✢ ✢ ✢

Why do cows have bells round their necks?

IN CASE THEIR HORNS DON'T WORK.

✢ ✢ ✢

WHICH IS THE FASTEST FISH IN THE WATER?

THE MOTOR PIKE.

✢ ✢ ✢ ✢ ✢

Which side of a bear has the most fur?

THE OUTSIDE.

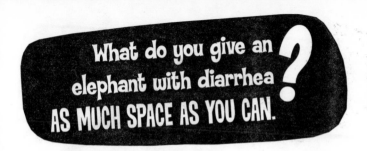

What do you give an elephant with diarrhea? AS MUCH SPACE AS YOU CAN.

What goes, **'CLUCK-PECK! CLUCK-PECK! CLUCK-PECK! BOOM!!'?**

A chicken in a minefield.

WHAT GOES BLACK-WHITE-BLACK-WHITE-BLACK-WHITE?

TWO PENGUINS FIGHTING OVER A HOT WATER BOTTLE.

What do you get if you cross an **ELEPHANT** with the abominable snowman?

A JUMBO YETI.

WHICH FISH DRESSES LIKE A GANGSTER?

Al Caprawn.

WHY DID THE ONE-EYED CHICKEN CROSS THE ROAD?
To get to the Birds Eye shop.

What do you get if you cross a PARROT with a SHARK?

A FISH that sits on your shoulder, bites your head off and then says,

'WHO'S A PRETTY BOY, THEN?'

What do you get if you cross a duck and a cat with a road roller?

A duck billed flatty puss.

Why did the homeless turtle cross the road?
TO GET TO THE SHELL STATION.

YOU HAVE A REFEREE IN FOOTBALL AND AN UMPIRE IN CRICKET, BUT WHAT DO YOU HAVE IN BOWLS?
GOLDFISH.

MRS WICKET WASN'T TOO WORRIED WHEN SCRAPPER SWALLOWED THREE POUND COINS. AT LEAST THERE WAS SOME MONEY IN THE KITTY.

When the old gorilla died at the zoo, the zoo was too short of money to buy a new one, so they hired an actor in a gorilla suit to sit in the cage and act like a gorilla. This all went well for the first couple of weeks, but then the actor started to get bored and began larking around, much like a real gorilla. Unfortunately, he went a bit too far one day when he was climbing the bars of his cage and he fell into the tiger's cage next door. The tiger immediately leapt across the cage.

'**Help!**' screamed the actor.
'**Get me out of here!**'
'**Shut up,**' said the tiger. '**Do you want to get us both sacked?**'

Mother octopus was serving lunch and the kids were really getting on her nerves.

'HURRY UP, MUM!' they shouted.

'WE'RE STARVING!'

'OH, GIVE ME A BREAK!' snapped Mother octopus.

'I'VE ONLY GOT FOUR PAIRS OF HANDS!'

WHY IS THE RHINOCEROS COVERED IN WRINKLES? Have you ever tried ironing one?

HOW DO YOU STOP A RHINOCEROS CHARGING? CANCEL HIS CREDIT CARDS.

What do you call a deer with no eyes?

NO EYE DEER.

✤ ✤ ✤ ✤ ✤ ✤ ✤ ✤ ✤ ✤ ✤

WHAT GOES BLACK-WHITE-BLACK-WHITE-BLACK-WHITE?

A PENGUIN STUCK IN A REVOLVING DOOR.

✤ ✤ ✤ ✤ ✤ ✤ ✤ ✤ ✤ ✤ ✤

What do you call a deer with no eyes and no legs?

STILL NO EYE DEER.

WHAT DO YOU CALL A FISH WITHOUT AN EYE? A FSH.

HOW MANY WET LABRADORS DOES IT TAKE TO STINK THE ROOM OUT?
A phew!

How can you find out the age of a tortoise?

LOOK IN HIS PASSPORT.

❖ ❖ ❖ ❖ ❖ ❖ ❖ ❖ ❖ ❖ ❖

WHY did the duck run onto the football pitch?

BECAUSE THE REFEREE BLEW FOR A FOWL.

❖ ❖ ❖ ❖ ❖ ❖ ❖ ❖ ❖

What do **YOU** call a woodpecker with no beak?

A HEADBANGER.

What's the difference between a buffalo and a bison?
YOU CAN'T WASH YOUR HANDS IN A BUFFALO.

• • • • • • • • • • • • • • • • • • •

What goes BOING! **ROAR!** BOING!
ROAR! BOING! **ROAR!**

A LION on a pogo stick.

• • • • • • • • • • • •  • • • • • • • • • •

How do fleas get from dog to dog?
BY ITCHING A LIFT.

• • • • • • • • • • • • • • • • • • •

How do you know when your cat has eaten a duck?

HE'S A LITTLE DOWN IN THE MOUTH.

A man was driving home late one night when a cat dashed out in front of his car. Unfortunately, he had no way of avoiding it and the cat was run over and killed. The man stopped his car and looked at the poor cat's collar. The owner's address was on a collar tag, and he was right outside the house, so he knocked on the door. A little old lady answered.

'I'M MOST AWFULLY SORRY,' said the man, 'BUT YOUR CAT RAN OUT IN FRONT OF MY CAR AND I'VE KILLED HIM. I'M MORE THAN WILLING TO REPLACE HIM, IF YOU LIKE.'

'OKAY,' said the old lady, 'BUT HOW ARE YOU AT CATCHING MICE?'

WEDNESDAY JOKES

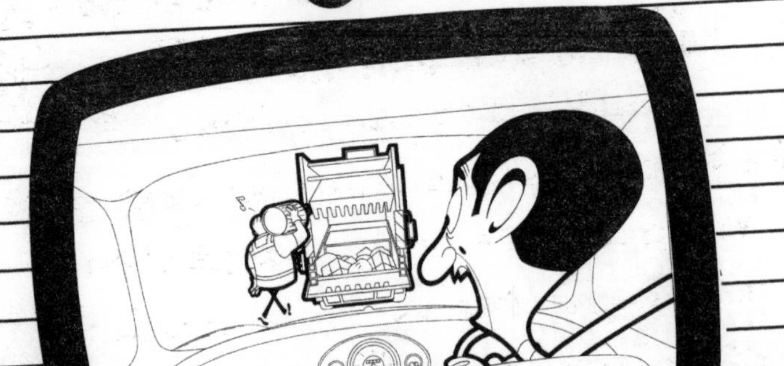

Wednesday is the **RUBBISH DAY**. I don't mean that it's any worse than any other day, it's just the day the **BIN MEN** come. As it's the day the bin men are here, Mrs Wicket likes to make it the day when she asks all sorts of workmen to come – plumbers, joiners, electricians, builders. Maybe it's because Mrs Wicket's house is so old –

IT'S EVEN OLDER THAN HER

– that it has so many problems.

Mrs Wicket always blames me when things go wrong but that's just her little joke. She never laughs when she says it, though. In fact, I've never seen her laugh at all. Maybe I should try some of these Wednesday jokes on her. Mrs Wicket might not laugh very often but you'll laugh yourself bonkers when you read these Wednesday jokes. Wrap bandages around your ribs and keep your doctor's phone number handy in case you **SPLIT YOUR SIDES!!**

A WOMAN went to the doctor with a pimple on her face with a tree growing out of it. Beside the tree were some bushes and a picnic table and four chairs. **'Don't worry,'** said the doctor. **'It's only a beauty spot.'**

Mrs Wicket was very annoyed to see an electrician walking up towards the front door.

'What are you doing here today?' she ranted as she opened the door. **'You were supposed to come and fix the doorbell yesterday.'**

'I did come yesterday,' said the electrician. **'I rang the bell a dozen times but there was nobody in.'**

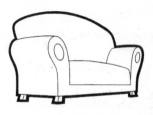

A MAN went to his **doctor and said**, 'Doctor, you've got to help me. I keep thinking I'm a labrador.'

'Really?' **said the doctor.** 'Go over there and lie on the couch.'

'I can't,' **said the man.** 'I'm not allowed on the furniture.'

WOOF!

WHAT HAS TWO LEGS AND FLIES?

A bin man's trousers.

WHAT'S THE BEST WAY TO GET RID OF VARNISH?

Drop the 'r' to make it **VANISH.**

What's worse than raining cats and dogs?

Hailing taxis.

WHISTLING A MERRY TUNE, THE DUSTBIN MAN WAS WALKING TOWARDS THE BIN LORRY WITH THREE FULL DUSTBINS BALANCED ON HIS HEAD AND ONE UNDER EACH ARM. **'GOSH,'** SAID A PASSER-BY. **'That looks really difficult. How on earth do you manage it?'**

'It's not too hard,' SAID THE BIN MAN. 'You just make a shape with your lips and **BLOW**.'

What's black **and smelly and hangs from the ceiling?**
AN UNLUCKY ELECTRICIAN.

What looks like half a cat?
THE OTHER HALF.

Mrs Wicket took Scrapper to the vet.
'He's being impossible,' **said Mrs Wicket.** 'He chases anyone on a skateboard. What do you think I should do?'
'Well,' **said the vet.** 'You could take away his skateboard.'

ZOOM!

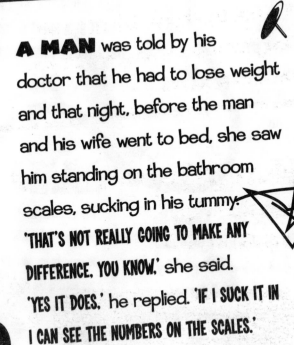

A MAN was told by his doctor that he had to lose weight and that night, before the man and his wife went to bed, she saw him standing on the bathroom scales, sucking in his tummy.
'THAT'S NOT REALLY GOING TO MAKE ANY DIFFERENCE, YOU KNOW,' she said.
'YES IT DOES,' he replied. 'IF I SUCK IT IN I CAN SEE THE NUMBERS ON THE SCALES.'

DOCTOR!

Doctor, doctor, my husband thinks he's a BMW.
Well send him in. I can't, he's been clamped outside.

Doctor, doctor, I still keep acting
like a clock. Don't get so wound up.

DOCTOR, DOCTOR,
I FEEL LIKE A
PACK OF CARDS.
STOP SHUFFLING
AROUND AND
I'LL DEAL WITH
YOU LATER.

DOCTOR, DOCTOR, I STILL
KEEP ACTING LIKE A CLOCK.
MUST BE A SWISS CLOCK.
WHY? YOU'RE GOING CUCKOO.

Doctor, doctor, I've swallowed a cricket ball. How's that? Oh, don't you start, too.

Doctor, doctor, I must be
seeing things. i just saw
a man being mugged by
a six-foot-tall insect.
Yes, there's a nasty bug
going around.

Doctor, doctor, my
husband has been acting
like a chicken for the
past year. Why didn't
you come to me sooner?
We needed the eggs.

DOCTOR!

Doctor, doctor, my husband thinks he's a bird. Well send him in. I can't, he's flown south for the winter.

Well, is there anything I can take for it? Well, you could start with my hat and umbrella.

Doctor, doctor, I'm getting smaller and smaller every day. I can't give you an appointment till next Wednesday. But I'll have shrunk loads by then. Well, you'll just have to be a little patient.

Doctor, doctor, I can't pronounce my Fs, Ts or Hs. Well, you can't say fairer than that then.

Doctor, doctor, I think I'm a coat stand

DOCTOR, DOCTOR, I FEEL LIKE A PAIR OF CURTAINS! PULL YOURSELF TOGETHER, MAN!

DOCTOR, DOCTOR, I KEEP ACTING LIKE A CLOCK. THERE'S NO CAUSE FOR ALARM.

Doctor, doctor, I keep forgetting things. How long have you had this problem? What problem?

What does Moby Dick do on his birthday? HE HAS A WHALE OF A TIME.

Why did the chewing gum cross the road? **It was stuck to the chicken's foot.**

A man applied for a job as a handyman and was asked for an interview.

'WHAT SKILLS DO YOU HAVE?' asked the interviewer.

'NONE, REALLY,' said the man.

'THEN WHAT MAKES YOU THINK YOU'RE A HANDYMAN?' asked the interviewer.

'WELL, I ONLY LIVE ROUND THE CORNER ...'

Did you hear about the archaeologist who got all upset because his career was in ruins?

● ● ● ● ● ● ● ●

The baby elephant was really worried. His trunk was eleven inches long and he was frightened that it would grow into a foot.

A MAN went to his doctor with an unusual complaint. 'DOCTOR,' said the man, 'EVERYBODY THINKS I'M CRAZY JUST BECAUSE I LIKE GRAPES.'

'THAT'S SILLY,' said the doctor. 'I LIKE GRAPES, TOO.'

'REALLY?' said the man. 'WOULD YOU LIKE TO COME AND SEE MY COLLECTION?'

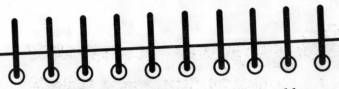

A WORKMAN went into a tool hire shop and asked for the best chain saw they had because he had to chop down six trees that morning. The assistant gave him their best model of chain saw and assured him that it would do the job. At lunchtime the workman returned with the chainsaw.

'I only managed to cut down one tree,' he said. 'You promised that this chain saw would get through six.'

'I don't understand,' said the shop assistant. 'This is the most efficient chain saw we have. Let me take a look at it.'

The shop assistant took the chain saw, and pulled the cord to start it up.

'What's that noise?' said the workman.

A MAN WALKED INTO HIS DOCTOR'S SURGERY BACKWARDS, PULLING HIS ARMS BACKWARDS AND FORWARDS.

'What on earth are you doing?' **ASKED THE DOCTOR.**

'I'm rowing this boat,' **SAID THE MAN.**

'But there's no boat there!' **SAID THE DOCTOR.**

'Help! Help! I can't swim!!'

✦ ✦ ✦ ✦ ✦ ✦ ✦ ✦ ✦

A woman went to see her doctor with a nasty burn all down one side of her face.

'HOW DID YOU DO THAT?' asked the doctor.

'IT'S JUST ME BEING ABSENT-MINDED,' said the woman.

'WHY, WHAT HAPPENED?' the doctor asked.

'SOMEONE PHONED WHILE I WAS IRONING.'

What do you call the girl who stands behind the goal at football practice?

Annette.

What do you call a workman with a spade on his head?

DUG.

WHAT DO YOU CALL A WORKMAN WITHOUT A SPADE ON HIS HEAD?

DUGLESS.

What do you call a mechanic with a car on his head?

JACK.

WHAT DO YOU CALL A PLUMBER WITH A TOILET ON HIS HEAD?

Lou.

WHAT DO YOU CALL A FEMALE PLUMBER WITH TWO TOILETS ON HER HEAD?

 Lulu.

What do you call a man with a lighthouse on his head?

Cliff.

What do you call a workman called Richard with a road roller on his head?

FLATRICK.

Why do policemen have numbers? IN CASE THEY GET LOST.

❧ ❧ ❧

A builder was excavating a site when he came across three ancient holes in the ground. **WELL, WELL, WELL.**

A LITTLE BOY walked past an allotment where a gardener was hard at work. The boy was **DISGUSTED** to see the gardener carrying a bucketful of steaming **DUNG**.

'What are you going to do with that?' he asked.

'I'm going to spread it on my strawberries,' answered the gardener.

'YUK!' howled the little boy.

'We have cream on ours!'

A workman called to mend a broken window. He examined the glass, sighed and said, 'YES, IT'S A BAD ONE, ALL RIGHT. BROKEN ON BOTH SIDES.'

A workman walked into his doctor's surgery. 'I know what's wrong with you,' the doctor immediately said. 'You've got a sore stomach.' 'Well, yes I do,' said the workman. 'How did you know that?'

'Anyone who accidentally ate his pencil at breakfast time is going to have a sore stomach,' said the doctor.

'What makes you think I ate a pencil?' asked the workman.

'You have a sausage behind your ear.'

Slurp!

Thursday is a really loud day. It takes its name from the mystical ancient English god, Thunor, the god of thunder, which was the same as Thor, the thunder god of the Norse. 'What's a Norse?' I hear you ask.

'It's a big friendly animal with a jockey on its back,' I say. **HA-HA!** No, the Norse were ancient Scandinavian people, like the Viking raiders who used to attack the coast of Britain in their longboats, the rotters! Those were dark and gloomy days indeed for poor old Britain. There's no need for all that dark and gloomy nonsense now though and the only way anything Scandinavian is going to do you any harm is if you get run over by a Volvo. But let's keep Thursday **LOUD!!** Tell these Thursday jokes in a **LOUD** voice and then laugh

EVEN LOUDER!!

A general had a new computer in his headquarters. He decided to ask it a question and typed in:

'How far away is the enemy?'

'Seven hundred' appeared on the computer screen.

'Seven hundred what?' typed in the General and the screen read:

'Seven hundred, sir!'

CAN A SHOE BOX?
No, but a tin can.

What's half of infinity?
Nity.

What's Dracula's favourite sport?
BATMINTON.

Which is fastest, COLD or **HEAT?**
HEAT, you can catch COLD.

**What's brown and sticky?
A STICK.**

A LITTLE BOY WAS CRYING AND WHEN HIS MUM
ASKED HIM WHY HE SAID:
'My new trainers are hurting.'
'That's because you've put
them on the wrong feet,'
his mum explained.
'But these are the only
feet I have!'

**WHERE DO WHALES GO TO
CHECK THEIR WEIGHT?**
THE WHALE WEIGH STATION.

THREE SOLDIERS, AN ENGLISHMAN,
A SCOTSMAN AND AN IRISHMAN
WERE CAPTURED BY THE ENEMY AND PUT IN
FRONT OF A FIRING SQUAD. AS THE FIRING
SQUAD TOOK AIM, THE ENGLISHMAN
SHOUTED 'AVALANCHE!!'
THE FIRING SQUAD ALL LOOKED UP AT THE
HILLSIDE AND THE ENGLISHMAN MADE HIS
GETAWAY WHILE THEIR BACKS WERE TURNED.
THEN THEY TOOK AIM ONCE AGAIN AND THE
SCOTSMAN SHOUTED 'FLOOD!!'
THE FIRING SQUAD ALL LOOKED DOWN
TO THE RIVER AND THE SCOTSMAN
MADE HIS GETAWAY WHILE THEIR
BACKS WERE TURNED. THEN THEY
TOOK AIM ONCE AGAIN AND THE
IRISHMAN SHOUTED 'FIRE!!'

Ha Ha Ha

How do you keep an idiot in suspense?

Which criminal mastermind lives under the sea?

THE CODFATHER.

What do you always see at the end of everything?

g

What's pink and fluffy?
Pink fluff.

What's blue and fluffy?
Pink fluff holding its breath.

I'll tell you tomorrow.

What do they do when there's a burglary under the sea?
Send for the plaice.

DID you hear about the YACHTSMAN who caught FIRE?
HE was wearing a BLAZER.

WHAT starts with e and ends with e but has only one letter in it?
Envelope!

What's an IG?
An eskimo's house with no loo.

WHAT WORD DO WE ALWAYS PRONOUNCE WRONG?
WRONG.

What's rosy pink but
close to silver?
THE LONE RANGER'S BUM.

✧ ✧ ✧ ✧ ✧

Did you hear the
one about the
contagious disease**?**
You'd probably
get it
straight away.

✧ ✧ ✧ ✧ ✧

**DID YOU HEAR ABOUT
THE BURGLAR WHO
BROKE INTO A BAKER'S SHOP AND ATE
17 PRUNE TARTS?**
He was on the run for days.

WHAT WAS THE SNAIL DOING ON THE MOTORWAY?
LESS THAN 1 MILE AN HOUR!

Two soldiers, a corporal and a private, were mending the perimeter fence around the army camp. The corporal looked at the damaged fence.

'Okay,' he said to the private. 'I need you to get me six planks of wood, two boxes of nails and a namafor.'

'What's a namafor?' asked the private.

'It's for banging the nails in, stupid!'

What is the DIFFERENCE between a soldier and a policeman?

YOU CAN'T DIP A POLICEMAN IN YOUR EGG!

TWO BOYS WHOSE FATHERS WERE IN THE NAVY WERE ARGUING ABOUT WHICH OF THEIR DADS WAS STRONGEST.

'You know the Atlantic Ocean?' SAID THE FIRST BOY. 'Well my dad dug the hole for it in just one afternoon.'

'**THAT'S NOTHING**,' SAID THE SECOND BOY. 'YOU KNOW THE DEAD SEA? MY DAD STRANGLED IT WITH HIS BARE HANDS!'

'I THINK YOUR SON IS HORRIBLY SPOILED,' an old lady said to a proud mother one day. 'DON'T BE RIDICULOUS!' snapped the boy's mum. 'MY SON'S A PERFECT LITTLE GENT.' 'AH, BUT YOU HAVEN'T SEEN WHAT THE STEAMROLLER'S DONE TO HIM!'

How do you know when an elephant has been sleeping in your bed?

The sheets are wrinkled and there are peanut crumbs on the pillow.

HOW DO YOU KNOW WHEN AN ELEPHANT IS HIDING UNDER YOUR BED?

Your nose is scraping the ceiling.

How do you know when an elephant is still sleeping in your bed?
He has an E on his pyjamas.

WHAT'S BLUE, HAS BIG EARS AND A LONG NOSE?

AN ELEPHANT HOLDING ITS BREATH.

Why do the elephants have **BIG EARS**?
BECAUSE NODDY WON'T PAY THE RANSOM.

WHAT'S LARGE, GREY AND CAN TAKE OFF VERTICALLY?
AN ELECOPTER.

WHAT'S BIG AND GREY AND TERRORISES THE THEATRE ?
The **ELEPHANTOM** of the Opera.

Why were the elephants thrown out of the swimming baths?

They wouldn't keep their trunks up!

TWO SOLDIERS WERE HAVING LUNCH WHEN ONE ASKED THE OTHER TO PASS THE CHOCOLATE CAKE.

'Sorry,' **said his friend.** 'I can't do that.'

'Why not?' **asked the first soldier.**

'Because it's against regulations to help another soldier to dessert.'

✤ ✤ ✤ ✤ ✤ ✤ ✤ ✤ ✤ ✤ ✤

DID YOU HEAR ABOUT THE 2 AERIALS THAT GOT MARRIED?
THE CEREMONY WASN'T UP TO MUCH BUT THE RECEPTION WAS EXCELLENT.

✤ ✤ ✤ ✤ ✤ ✤ ✤ ✤ ✤ ✤ ✤

Where do little fish go when their mummies and daddies are at work?
PLAICE SCHOOL.

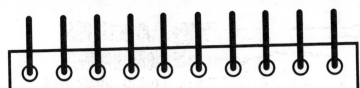

A soldier was making his first ever parachute jump. He was falling through the air and pulled the cord to open his parachute. It came off in his hand. Trying not to panic, he pulled the cord on his spare parachute. NOTHING happened. Just then he hurtled down towards a man who was shooting upwards. The man was smoking a cigarette, holding a lighted match in one hand and a spanner in the other.

'EXCUSE ME,' said the soldier. 'DO YOU KNOW ANYTHING ABOUT PARACHUTES?'

'NO,' said the man as they passed in mid-air. 'DO YOU KNOW ANYTHING ABOUT GAS COOKERS?'

A general walked up to a private and asked:

'DO YOU HAVE CHANGE OF A **£10 NOTE?**'

'SURE, MATE,' said the private, rummaging in his pockets.

'JUST HANG ON A MINUTE, PAL.'

'THAT'S NO WAY TO SPEAK TO AN OFFICER!' roared the general.

'NOW DO YOU HAVE CHANGE OF A **£10 NOTE?**'

'NO, SIR!'

The small, shy pebble soldier had just one wish in the world.

To be a little boulder.

WHICH OF KING ARTHUR'S KNIGHTS INVENTED THE ROUND TABLE?

Sir Cumference.

A SOLDIER man was walking along whistling, with a roll of barbed wire balanced on his head, ONE ON EACH SHOULDER AND AN OIL DRUM UNDER EACH ARM.

'How on earth do you do that?' ASKED A PASSING OFFICER.

'It's easy,' replied the soldier, 'just put your lips together and blow'.

• • • • • • • • • • • • •

A SOLDIER RUSHED IN TO SEE THE MEDICAL OFFICER.

'YOU'VE GOT TO HELP ME, SIR,' he said. 'I HAVE CABBAGES GROWING IN MY EARS!'

'Incredible,' **said the medical officer.** 'I've no idea how that could have happened.'

'NEITHER DO I,' said the soldier. 'I PLANTED POTATOES!'

!

WHAT do you call a Viking wearing paper undies?

RUSSELL.

HOW DID VIKING SHIPS COMMUNICATE WITH EACH OTHER? By NORSE code.

HOW do you stop a Viking wrecking the back of your car? Let him sit in the front.

WHAT DO YOU CALL A VIKING FLOATING IN THE WATER?

BOB.

WHAT'S blonde and hums?

A DEAD VIKING.

WHAT DO YOU CALL A VIKING WEARING A PLASTIC COAT?

MAC.

DID you hear about Marks and Spencer the two plundering Viking thieves?

They were a pair of nickers.

WHAT do YOU call a Viking wearing two plastic coats?

MAX

THERE WAS ONCE A FAMILY OF ENORMOUS VIKINGS. MR BIGGER, MRS BIGGER AND THEIR SON, BABY BIGGER. WHICH OF THEM DO YOU THINK WAS THE BIGGEST?

BABY BIGGER - HE WAS JUST A LITTLE BIGGER.

Why was six scared of seven.

He'd heard people say

SEVEN ATE NINE.

WHAT'S THE WORLD'S LONGEST WORD?
SMILES - THERE'S A MILE BETWEEN
THE BEGINNING AND THE END!

WHY COULDN'T THE SKELETON

CROSS THE ROAD?

He didn't have the guts.

HOW MANY SECONDS ARE THERE IN A YEAR?
TWELVE - JANUARY 2ND, FEBRUARY 2ND,
MARCH 2ND ...

HOW DOES THE ABOMINABLE SNOWMAN GO TO THE SHOPS?

BY ICICLE.

Where is the best place to find hippies?
AT THE TOP OF YOUR LEGGIES.

TWO FLEAS MET IN ROBINSON CRUSOE'S BEARD. THEY HAD A BIT OF A CHAT BEFORE ONE HOPPED OFF. **'CHEERIO!'** he shouted. **'SEE YOU ON FRIDAY.'**

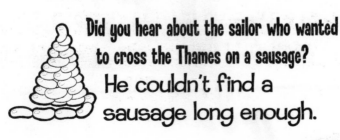

Did you hear about the sailor who wanted to cross the Thames on a sausage?
He couldn't find a sausage long enough.

A young soldier was about to go into
battle when he realised that he had
forgotten his rifle.
'Never mind,' said the sergeant.
'People get so excited during a battle
that you can frighten them to death.
Just point this stick at them and shout
"Bangity-Bangity-Bangity!" and the
enemy will be scared stiff.
'But what about my bayonet?' said the
young soldier. 'It was with my rifle.'
'Never mind,' said the sergeant. 'Just
take this twig and wave it at them and
shout "Stabbity-Stabbity-Stabbity!" and
the enemy will be terrified of you.'
Sure enough, when the young soldier
found himself in a tight spot on the
battlefield, with the enemy running

towards him, he pointed his stick and shouted 'Bangity-Bangity-Bangity' and most of the enemy either fainted with terror or ran away. When some still came charging on, he whipped out his twig and screamed, 'Stabbity-Stabbity-Stabbity!' and most of the rest ran off, until there was just one enemy soldier walking slowly towards him. He ignored all of the young soldier's shouting, walked right up to him, knocked him down and walked over him, mumbling, 'Tankity-Tankity-Tankity.'

FRIDAY Jokes

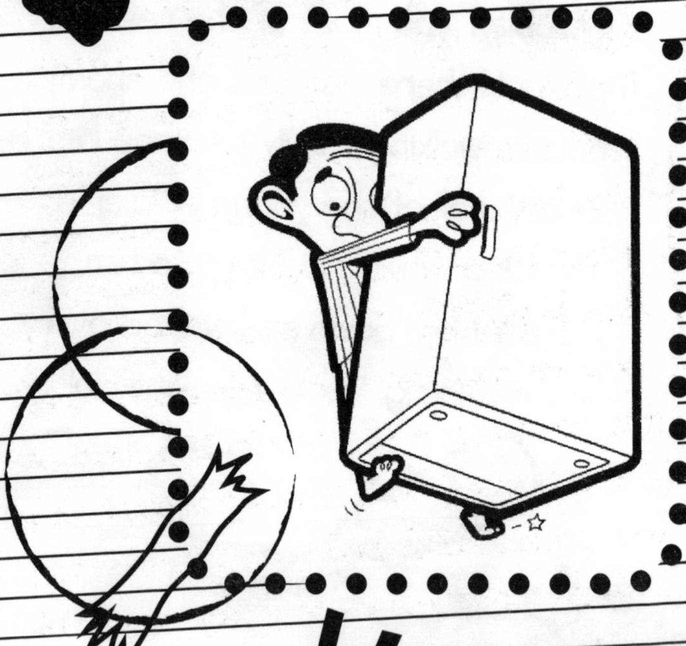

Waiter!

Friday is a **BRILLIANT DAY**.

It's the start of the weekend and everybody is happy because the school week (or the working week if you have a job) is almost over. You can have a lie-in on Saturday morning, so Friday night is a good night to stay up late or go out to dinner - the **FRIDGE** in my flat is usually looking pretty foodless by the time Friday comes around.

With everybody in such a cheerful mood, what better time to try them out with a few jokes. These Friday jokes will obviously be ideal. **WARNING!** Telling people jokes about how horrible restaurants are just before they go out for a meal on a Friday evening is a risky business likely to result in you losing your pocket money, being grounded, getting a clout round the earhole or any manner of upleasant things.

PROCEED WITH CAUTION!!!

A snail **SLITHERED** into a restaurant on a Friday night and asked for a table for one.

'GET OUT OF HERE!' yelled the waiter, picking up the snail. 'WE DON'T WANT SNAILS IN HERE.' And he threw the snail out the door and right across the road.

THE NEXT FRIDAY THE SNAIL CAME SLITHERING IN AGAIN AND SAID TO THE WAITER: **'WHAT DID YOU DO THAT FOR?'**

A man went into a pub with a lump of tarmac under his arm and said: 'Can i have a lager, please, and one for the road?'

HOW DO YOU GET AN ELEPHANT UP AN OAK TREE? **Tell him to sit on an** acorn and wait for it to grow.

How do you get an elephant down from an oak tree? Tell him to sit on a leaf and wait for the fall.

What's blue and square? An orange in disguise.

WHY DID THE **RAISIN** ASK THE PRUNE TO GO TO THE **CINEMA**? BECAUSE HE COULDN'T FIND A **DATE**.

A BOY walked into a chip shop with a lizard on his shoulder. 'What's that?' **asked the assistant behind the counter.** 'This is Tiny,' **said the boy.** 'Why do you call him Tiny?' **the assistant asked.** 'Because he's my newt!'

What is covered in wrapping paper and flies**?**

A birthday pheasant.

WHAT DO YOU CALL A FLY WITH NO WINGS?
A WALK.

Where do you get monster snails?
ON MONSTERS' FINGERS.

What's the best thing to put in a pizza? **YOUR TEETH.**

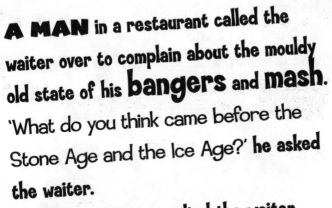

A MAN in a restaurant called the waiter over to complain about the mouldy old state of his **bangers** and **mash**.

'What do you think came before the Stone Age and the Ice Age?' he asked the waiter.

'I don't know, Sir,' replied the waiter.

The man pointed to his plate.

'THE SAUSAGE!'

A FRENCH CHEF who prided himself on serving only the freshest of food in his restaurant sent the youngest of his trainees out to the market to buy some **SNAILS**.

The trainee set off for the market, fell asleep on the bus, missed his stop and took two hours to find his way back to the market. He bought all of the snails that were left and was given a bucket to carry them back to the restaurant.

Unfortunately, he fell asleep on the bus again and took another two hours to make his way back to the restaurant. As he hurried up the restaurant's front steps, he slipped and spilled the bucket of snails all the way down the stairs.

The chef heard the commotion and threw open the door. **'WHERE HAVE YOU BEEN?'** he roared. 'HOW DO YOU EXPECT ME TO SERVE THE FRESHEST OF FOOD IF YOU TAKE SO LONG TO GET HERE?'

The trainee looked at the snails spilled all the way down the stairs and yelled: **'COME ON, GUYS! WE'RE ALMOST THERE!'**

'Coffee, please,' said the man in the restaurant.
'Without cream.'
'We haven't got any cream,' said the waitress.
'Would you like it without milk, instead?'

Moooo

DID YOU HEAR ABOUT THE BUTCHER'S BOY
WHO SAT ON THE BACON SLICER?
He got a **LITTLE BEHIND**
in his deliveries.

What's big and grey and leaves
the party early? Cinderellephant.

What's the strongest of all
shellfish? **THE MUSCLE.**

A girl was at the cinema with her boyfriend when she noticed a man come to sit beside them with a crocodile on a lead. The man and the **CROCODILE** sat down to watch the film and tucked into some popcorn.

'EXCUSE ME,' said the girl, 'BUT I HAVE TO SAY THAT I'M A BIT SHOCKED TO SEE A CROCODILE IN HERE WATCHING THE FILM.'

'I'm a bit surprised myself,' said the man. 'He hated the book.'

Ha Two cannibals were eating a clown. One said to the other, 'Does this taste funny to you?'

WAITER!

Waiter! This fish looks like it's sleeping on my chips! Well, it is a kipper, Sir.

WAITER, DO YOU SERVE CRABS? YES, SIR, WE SERVE ANYONE.

WAITER! THERE'S A FLY IN MY WINE. WELL, YOU DID ASK FOR SOMETHING WITH A LITTLE BODY IN IT, SIR.

Waiter, get your thumb off my steak! You don't want me to drop it again, do you?

Waiter, what's this fly doing sliding down my ice cream? Learning to ski, sir.

Waiter! Waiter! I've just swallowed a fish bone. Are you choking, sir? No, I'm totally serious!

A man and a woman went out one **FRIDAY** for a rare visit to a restaurant and the woman was appalled by her husband's manners.

'IF YOU MUST YAWN,' she hissed at him, 'PUT YOUR HAND OVER YOUR MOUTH!'

'**No way!**' said the husband. '**I might get bitten!**'

What KIND OF NUTS HAVE HAY FEVER? CASHEWS.

In a posh restaurant, which hand should you use to stir your tea? Neither, use a **SPOON** for goodness sake!

Why was the brush
late for work?

it over swept.

 How do you start
a flea race?

ONE, TWO, FLEA, GO!

WHAT KIND OF MERINGUES
CAN'T YOU THROW AWAY?

BOOMERINGUES.

 What do you use in a
jungle birthday cake?

TARZIPAN.

WHAT DO YOU GIVE AN INJURED LEMON?

Lemonaid.

WHAT CAN A WHOLE LEMON DO THAT HALF A LEMON CAN'T?

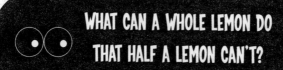

Look round.

What do you call a Scottish cloakroom assistant?

Angus McOatup.

What do you call a snowman in the desert?

A PUDDLE.

Why aren't they growing bananas any longer?
Because they were long enough already.

• • • • •

What is long, bendy, yellow and costs **£1,000?** A BANANA. THE **£1,000** WAS A LIE.

• • • •

What's soft and yellow and smells of banana? Monkey puke. *Yuk!*

• • • •

HOW DO YOU MAKE A SHEPHERD'S PIE?
FIRST PEEL ONE SHEPHERD ...

What's green
and miserable?
Apple grumble.

What happened to the indian chef who slipped and dropped a curry pot on his head? He was in a korma.

What is soft on the top, crispy on the bottom, stands 50 metres tall, is covered in cheese, tomatoes and onions and looks like it's about to fall over?

THE LEANING TOWER OF PIZZA.

A man went to a fancy dress party with a girl on his back.
'WHAT HAVE YOU COME AS?' ASKED THE HOST.
'A snail,' said the man.
'SO WHY DO YOU HAVE A GIRL ON YOUR BACK?'
'That's Michelle.'

Ha Ha Ha

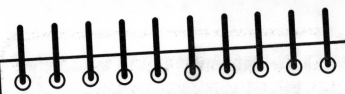

Every morning a man passed a house on his way to work and through the open window he could see a woman hitting her son over the head with a French loaf. One morning when he passed, there was something different. She was hitting the boy over the head with a large cake.

'Excuse me,' said the man, leaning through the window. **'But every morning I walk past and you are hitting that boy over the head with a French loaf and today you are bashing him with a cake. Why?'**
'WELL,' said the woman, 'IT IS HIS BIRTHDAY, AFTER ALL.'

DID YOU HEAR ABOUT THE DUCK WHO WAS SENT OFF DURING THE FOOTBALL MATCH FOR USING FOWL LANGUAGE?

Quack!

What's the difference between snot bogeys and sprouts? Kids won't eat sprouts.

A man walked into a bar —

'OUCH!'

A BOY went with his parents to stay in an ancient country mansion. In the middle of the night, he met a ghost in the corridor. 'I have been haunting these corridors for three centuries,' moaned the ghost.

'Oh, good,' said the boy. 'Can you tell me where the toilet is then?'

Booooooooo

Saturday Jokes

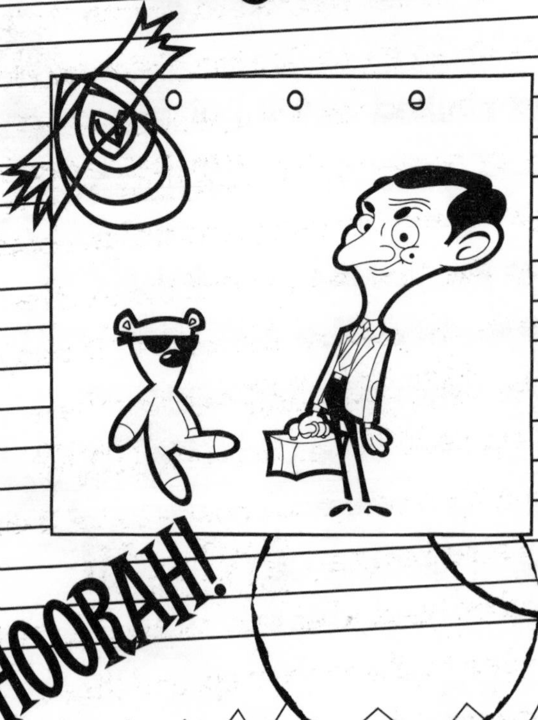

HOORAH!

Saturday is shopping day. **TEDDY** likes to sit at the front of the trolley when we go to the supermarket to remind me if I forget anything. He did once forget to remind me not to forget him, though, and I was half way home before I realised that I had left him in the trolley. Some people got very upset when I went back to the supermarket and had to search through their trollies to try to find him. Saturday also seems to be the day when people set off on holiday, or arrive at their **HOLIDAY HOTELS**.

You get asked the strangest things about holidays, like, 'How did you find the weather?' Well, it's usually just outside, isn't it? If people are so **SAD, SAD, SAD** that they have nothing better to do than ask **STUPID** questions, then somebody needs to tell them to stop being so **BORING!!** On the other hand, what they might need is a few jokes to cheer them up, and these Saturday jokes are just the ticket.

A lion and a tiger were walking down the High Street. The lion turned to the tiger and said: 'NOT MANY PEOPLE AROUND FOR A SATURDAY, ARE THERE?'

'SPECIAL OFFER TODAY!' called the man at the supermarket fish counter. '£10 BUYS YOU TWO HADDOCK, TWO PLAICE, HALF A SALMON AND A PANFOR!'
'WHAT'S A PANFOR?' asked a shopper. 'TO COOK THE FISH IN, STUPID.'

Where does Scrapper do his shopping?
IN A CAT-ALOGUE.

Did you hear about the bloke who spent two hours trying to get up the escalator in a department store. A notice said 'DOGS MUST BE CARRIED' and it took him ages to find one.

WHAT DO YOU GET IF YOU CROSS THE ATLANTIC WITH THE TITANIC?

About half way.

WHAT do you call an elephant at the top of Mount Everest?

LOST.

A British tourist was on a coach in California, chatting to an American in the seat next to her. 'WHERE ARE YOU HEADED FOR?' asked the American.

'SAN JOSE,' said the British woman.

'AH, YOU HAVEN'T PRONOUNCED THAT QUITE RIGHT,' said the American. 'IN CALIFORNIA WE PRONOUNCE THE JS LIKE HS, SO IT SOUNDS LIKE SAN HOSAY. HAVE YOU BEEN THERE BEFORE?'

'YES, said the British woman. 'I WAS THERE LAST HUNE AND HULY.'

Why was Cinderella dropped from the football team?
SHE KEPT RUNNING AWAY FROM THE BALL.

WHY DID CINDERELLA'S COACH FLOOD THE PITCH?
So he could bring on the sub.

. . . .

AND WHY WOULD CINDERELLA NEVER HAVE BEEN ANY GOOD AT FOOTBALL ANYWAY?
Her coach was a pumpkin.

Why does the Mississippi meander around so much?**?**

EVEN THOUGH IT HAS FOUR EYES, IT STILL CAN'T SEE.

DOES THE SEA SAY GOODBYE TO THE BEACH WHEN THE TIDE GOES OUT? **NO, BUT IT WAVES.**

WHICH French town has twin toilets?
TOULOUSE.

✤ ✤ ✤ ✤ ✤

WHICH FRENCH TOURIST ATTRACTION IS MADE FROM CUSTARD, JELLY, CREAM, SPONGE AND FRUIT?
THE TRIFLE TOWER.

✤ ✤ ✤ ✤ ✤

WHAT DID THE GRAPE DO WHEN THE ELEPHANT STOOD ON IT?

It gave a little wine.

Why do elephants have trunks?

Because they'd look silly in bikinis.

✤ ✤ ✤ ✤ ✤

WHAT'S the difference between an ELEPHANT and some nice, soft paper? YOU CAN'T WIPE YOUR BOTTOM WITH AN ELEPHANT.

✤ ✤ ✤ ✤ ✤ ✤

WHY DID THE FISH LOSE THEIR CRICKET MATCH AGAINST THE SHARKS? THEY LET THE GOLDFISH BOWL.

✤ ✤ ✤ ✤ ✤ ✤

HOW do you make a horse box? STICK HIM IN THE RING WITH MIKE TYSON.

A TOURIST WALKED INTO A COUNTRY VILLAGE PUB AND GOT TALKING TO AN OLD MAN. 'HAVE YOU LIVED HERE ALL YOUR LIFE?' ASKED THE TOURIST. 'NO,' SAID THE OLD MAN, 'NOT YET.'

A PLANE FULL OF TOURISTS WAS COMING IN TO LAND IN ATHENS IN WINTER WHEN AN OLD LADY CALLED THE STEWARDESS OVER AND POINTED TO THE WHITE-CAPPED HILLS OUTSIDE THE CITY.
'Excuse me, dear,' SAID THE OLD LADY. 'What's that down there?'
'That's snow, madam,' SAID THE STEWARDESS.
'Huh!' PUFFED THE WOMAN TURNING TO HER HUSBAND. 'You told me it was grease.'

WHAT'S grey and has a trunk?
A mouse going on holiday.

WHAT'S brown and has a trunk?
The mouse coming home again.

WHY DID THE DINOSAUR CROSS THE ROAD?

Because chickens weren't invented yet!

WHY DID THE DINOSAUR
CROSS THE PLAYGROUND?

To get to the other slide!

WHAT DO
DOLPHINS USE
TO GO ON HOLIDAY?

THE WHALE WAY.

DID you hear about the
HEDGEHOG who stormed out
of the supermarket?
He couldn't find the prickled
onions.

**Why does Mount Everest have such
good hearing?**
It has plenty of mountain ears.

THERE WAS ONCE A GREAT LION HUNTER IN AFRICA
WHO WAS FAMOUS FOR ALWAYS SHOOTING HIS PREY
RIGHT BETWEEN THE EYES. HE WOULD WAIT IN THE
MIDDLE OF A JUNGLE PATH AT NIGHT WHEN IT WAS
ABSOLUTELY DARK AND AIM BETWEEN THE TWO
LUMINOUS EYES OF THE LION. HE WAS EATEN BY TWO
ONE-EYED LIONS WALKING ARM-IN-ARM.

Two aliens were on holiday and visited our planet to find out more about humans.

'Some of the creatures on this planet don't eat meat,' **said one when they returned to their spaceship.** 'I spoke to one who said he had lived on vegetables for the last seven years.'

'Really?' **said the other.** 'I spoke to one who said he'd lived on earth his whole life.'

What comes out of the Thames and spreads fear over the East End of London?

JACK THE KIPPER.

WHERE DO SHARKS LIKE TO GO ON HOLIDAY?
Finland.

• •

A MAN WENT ON A HUNTING EXPEDITION IN CANADA, HOPING TO SPOT SOME BEAR TO PHOTOGRAPH. BEFORE THEY SET OUT FROM THEIR CAMP, HIS GUIDE GAVE HIM A BRIEFING.
'Have you ever hunted bear?' ASKED THE GUIDE.
'No,' SAID THE MAN, 'but I once went fishing in shorts.'

• • • • • • • • • • • • • • • • • • • •

WHAT WEARS A LONG COAT AND PANTS IN THE SUMMER? A DOG.

WHY do birds fly south for the winter?

Because it's too far to walk.

A duck was on holiday, fell asleep in the sun and got his face quite sunburned. He went into the chemist's shop in his hotel complex.

'Do you have anything for sunburn, please?' he asked the assistant.

'YOU COULD TRY THIS CREAM,' said the assistant. 'THAT SHOULD HELP.'

'Thank you,' said the duck. 'Could you put it on my bill?'

Out shopping for shoes, a man walked into a shoe shop.
'I'm looking for some crocodile shoes,' he said to the assistant.
'Certainly, sir,' said the assistant.
'What size is your crocodile?'

MRS WICKET once tried to wash her front doorstep, but she couldn't fit it into the washing machine.

A TOURIST LOOKED UP AT THE
LONDON EYE MILLENNIUM WHEEL.
'It's enormous,' HE SAID.
'Yes,' SAID A PASSER-BY, 'but you won't
believe the size of the hamster.'

A cowboy rode into town on
Friday, stayed for four days and
left on Friday. He rode for another
five days and arrived home on Friday.
How can this be?
HIS HORSE IS CALLED FRIDAY.

A WOMAN WENT INTO THE BUTCHER'S SHOP.
'I'd like a steak and kidley pie, please,'
SHE SAID.
'I think you mean steak and kidney pie,'
SAID THE BUTCHER.
'That's what I said, diddle I?'

At a swimming pool, a man climbed all the way up to the high diving board. He was about to dive when the lifeguard shouted, 'Don't dive - there's no water in that pool!'
'That's OK,' said the man.
'I can't swim!'

WHAT lives in the vegetable counter and holds up passing shoppers?
DICK TURNIP.

• • • • • • • • • • • • • • • • • • •

WHAT'S GREEN, LIVES IN THE VEGETABLE COUNTER AND SINGS ROCK 'N' ROLL?
Elvis Parsley.

• • • • • • • • • • • • • • • • • • •

WHAT'S BROWN AND HAIRY, WEARS SUNGLASSES AND CARRIES A SUITCASE.
A coconut going on holiday.

TWO yachtsmen were spending their holiday sailing from Portsmouth to New York. Somewhere out in the Atlantic, their boat struck an iceberg and sank. The two men managed to scramble out of the water and clung to the iceberg.

'We'll never survive out here,' gasped one.

'Yes we will,' said the other. 'Look, here comes the Titanic.'

A MAN WALKED INTO A HOTEL RECEPTION AREA.

'Can you give me a room and a bath?' HE ASKED.

'I can give you a room, sir,' SAID THE RECEPTIONIST, 'but you'll have to bath yourself.'

A boy started working in a butcher's shop on Saturday mornings. One of the older assistants there coughed one morning and his false teeth shot out into the mincing machine and were destroyed.

'Oh, no,' he moaned. 'Now i'll have to cancel my holiday to save up for new teeth.'

'Don't worry,' said the new boy. 'My dad will get me a set for you.'

Later that day, the new boy came back with the teeth, which fitted very well indeed.

'Fantastic!' said the man. 'Your dad must be a briliant dentist.'

'No,' replied the boy, 'He's an undertaker.'

> **Where are the Andes?**
> **ATTACHED TO YOUR WRISTIES.**

A MAN PHONED THE AIRPORT TO ASK ABOUT
FLIGHTS TO AUSTRALIA.

'How long does it take to get to
Australia?' HE ASKED.

'Just a minute,' SAID THE CLERK.

'Blimey, that's quick!'

✦ ✦ ✦ ✦ ✦ ✦ ✦ ✦ ✦

TWO sumo wrestlers went on a duck
hunting expedition with their
retriever dogs. The ducks flew
past in the sky but neither of the sumos got one.

'I KNOW WHAT'S WRONG,' said the first sumo.

'WHAT?' asked his friend.

'WE'RE NOT THROWING THE DOGS HIGH ENOUGH.'

SUNDAY Jokes

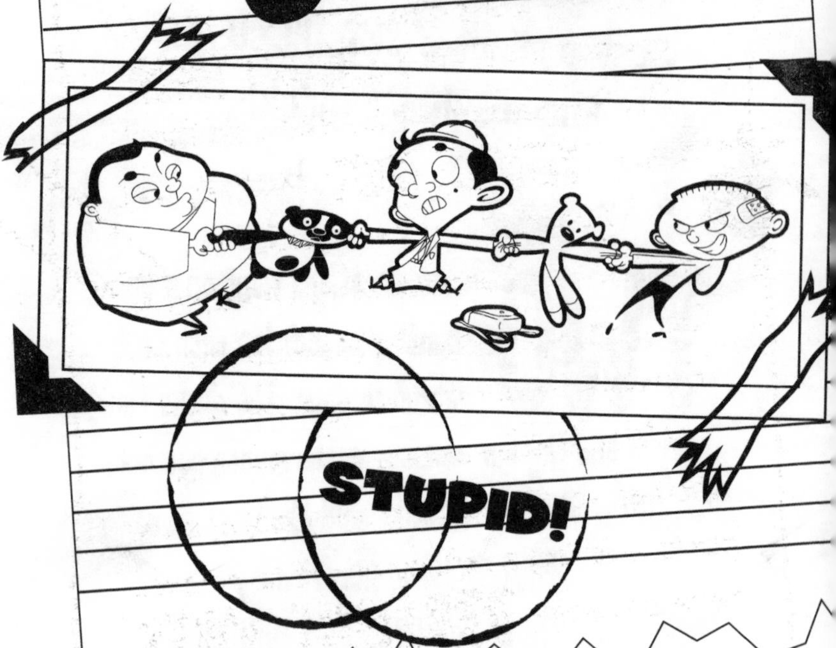

Sunday is the day for going to church and **WASHING THE CAR**. I don't go to church very often but my car's pretty clean. One of the things I always liked best about Sundays was Sunday school – especially the **SUNDAY SCHOOL PICNICS** when we would all go off into the countryside. I once really impressed all of the other boys and girls at Sunday school by setting a new world record for sitting in a **COW PAT**. They all said that I couldn't do it, but **I SHOWED THEM!** The Sunday school teacher said that I was a **'PERFECT IDIOT'** but I say that nobody's perfect. Sunday is another day associated with holidays. In fact, Sunday, being a holy day, is one of the days from which we get the word holiday. Holiday means 'holy day'. So, whether you're washing cars, going on a picnic, starting a holiday or off to church, here are some **BRILLIANT JOKES** to brighten up your day.

WHEN YOU'RE IN A FIELD HAVING A PICNIC,
WHAT DO YOU FIND THAT'S BROWN, SMELLY
AND SOUNDS LIKE A BELL?

DUNG.

What's the difference between a
Reliant Robin and a golf ball? You
can drive a golf
ball more than
200 metres.

❈ ❈ ❈ ❈ ❈

WHAT'S THE SILLIEST PLACE ON THE PLANET?

TWITZERLAND.

WHAT smashes into your
bedroom light at 150mph?
Stirling Moth.

WHY DID THE BULL RUSH?

Because it saw the cow slip.

Did you hear about the Reliant Robin with a faulty horn and no shame?

IT HAD A BREAKDOWN IN THE MIDDLE OF THE STREET AND COULDN'T GIVE A HOOT.

Mechanic: **Your car can't be much good at going up hills.**

Reliant Robin owner: **Well, yes and no.**

Mechanic: **What do you mean 'Yes and no?'**

Reliant Robin owner **Yes, it's no good at going up hills.**

Determined not to miss church on Sunday, a woman dressed up her son in his best clothes ready to go to Sunday school.

'But, Mum,' groaned the boy, 'I've got a really upset tummy.'

'Nonsense,' said his mother, 'you're just trying to get out of going to church.'

She marched him off to church. As they sat through the sermon prior to the children going into the Sunday school, she watched her son going strangely green about the face.

'What's wrong with you?'

whispered the mother.

'I think I'm gonna puke,' said the boy.

'Well for goodness sake do it outside,' his mother hissed.

The boy made for the door. Seconds later he was back, looking much better.

'You didn't throw up, then?' said his mother.

'Oh, yes,' said the boy, 'but I didn't have to go outside. They've got a box by the front door with a label on it that says, "For the sick."'

What do you call a Reliant Robin owner who is over six feet tall, bulging with muscles and carrying a machine gun?

SIR!

A vicar was Christening twin baby boys.
'AND WHAT IS THIS LITTLE LAD'S NAME?' he asked the mother.
'EDWARD,' replied the woman.
'AND HIS BROTHER'S NAME?' asked the vicar.
'EDWARD,' the mother replied.
'YOU'VE CALLED THEM BOTH EDWARD?' said the vicar, surprised.
'YES,' said the woman. 'TWO EDS ARE BETTER THAN ONE.'

On the Sunday school picnic, the vicar gave a lecture on plants and insects, telling all of the children that the colour red in nature usually stood for danger – a poisonous plant or stinging insect.

'So would you think that something with red and black stripes, big hairy legs and gnashing jaws was dangerous, Vicar?' asked one small boy.

'Yes,' said the vicar, 'that sounds very dangerous. Why do you ask?'

'Because I saw one going up your trouser leg!'

WHY DO TRAFFIC WARDENS HAVE YELLOW BANDS AROUND THEIR HATS?
To stop people parking on their heads.

A VICAR WENT ALONG TO THE AUDITIONS FOR A TELEVISION TALENT SHOW.
'WHAT DO YOU DO?' ASKED THE PRODUCER OF THE SHOW.
'BIRD IMPRESSIONS,' SAID THE VICAR.
'YOU MEAN A RANGE OF BIRD SONGS AND DIFFERENT BIRD CALLS?' ASKED THE PRODUCER.
'NO,' SAID THE VICAR. 'I EAT WORMS.'

HOW many days of the week begin with T?
All of them. I have milk and two sugars in mine.

FOR a perfect picnic in the park, how do you make a band stand?

STEAL THEIR CHAIRS.

WHAT kind of ants would really spoil your picnic?

ELEPHANTS.

WHAT kind of ants would eat all of your picnic and you, too?

GIANTS.

WHAT do you call a bloke on a picnic with six rabbits up his jumper?

WARREN.

THE SUNDAY

school teacher was leaving and the children all brought her presents on her last Sunday. The florist's daughter brought her a big bouquet of flowers. The baker's son brought her a beautiful cake. The son of the owner of the local off licence brought a big brown cardboard box. The teacher noticed something leaking out of the box. She tasted one of the drops.

'Is it a case of white wine?' she guessed.

'No,' said the little boy.

She tasted another drop.

'Is it a case of Champagne?' she guessed.

'No,' said the little boy.

'Brandy?' was her final guess from a third taste.

'No,' said the little boy.

'It's a puppy!'

WHAT TIME IS IT WHEN AN ELEPHANT SITS ON YOUR CAR?

Time to get a new car.

WHY WERE THE ELEPHANTS LAST TO BOARD NOAH'S ARK?

They had to pack their trunks.

WHAT'S the difference between a bird and a fly?

A BIRD CAN FLY BUT A FLY CAN'T BIRD.

⚜ ⚜ ⚜ ⚜ ⚜ ⚜ ⚜ ⚜ ⚜ ⚜

How can you tell which end of a worm is the head?

TICKLE ITS TUMMY AND SEE WHICH END LAUGHS.

A WORKMAN was repairing the stained glass window in the church when the vicar came along to see how he was doing. The workman climbed down off his ladder to admire his handiwork with the vicar.

'It looks very nice, but that piece of glass seems a bit loose,' said the vicar, pointing.

Just then the sheet of glass fell out of the window and chopped off the workman's ear.

'AAARGH!' howled the workman. 'THAT JUST CHOPPED ME EAR OFF!'

'Is this it?' asked the vicar, picking up an ear from the floor.

'DON'T THINK SO,' said the workman. 'MINE HAD A PENCIL BEHIND IT.'

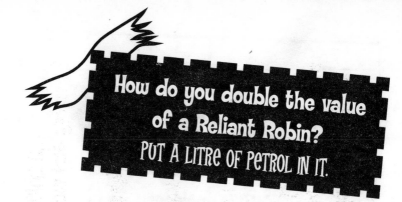

How do you double the value of a Reliant Robin?
PUT A LITRE OF PETROL IN IT.

Why does a Reliant Robin have a heated rear screen?
TO KEEP YOUR HANDS WARM WHEN YOU'RE PUSHING IT.

TARZAN picked up the jungle telephone and said, **'I want to talk to the King of Beasts.'**

'I'm sorry,' said a voice at the other end. **'I'm afraid the lion is busy.'**

A vicar

went to the zoo and accidentally fell into the TIGER'S enclosure. To his horror, the vicar saw a vicious and very hungry-looking tiger padding towards him, he FELL to his knees and prayed. SUDDENLY, the tiger knelt down, put his paws together and began praying, too.

'This is a miracle,' said the vicar to the tiger. 'I thought you were about to eat me but instead you have joined me in prayer.'

'SHUT UP,' said the tiger, **'I'M SAYING GRACE.'**

A LITTLE BOY WAS BOASTING TO A LITTLE GIRL THAT ON THE SUNDAY SCHOOL PICNIC HE HAD RUN AWAY FROM THE TEACHERS AND HID UNDER A COW.

'Really?' SAID THE LITTLE GIRL.

'Did you get a telling off?'

'No,' SAID THE LITTLE BOY,

'just a pat on the head.'

SPLAT!

WHY ARE AUNTIES LIKE A BOX OF CHOCOLATES? MOST OF THEM ARE QUITE SWEET BUT YOU DO GET A FEW NUTTY ONES.

WHY DID THE VICAR WALK INTO CHURCH ON HIS HANDS? It was Palm Sunday.

WHAT COMES IN A TUPPERWARE CONTAINER AND RINGS BELLS IN A FRENCH CATHEDRAL?

The lunchpack of Notre Dame.

A HUSBAND AND WIFE WERE HAVING A PICNIC IN THE COUNTRYSIDE. IT WAS BRILLIANT SUNSHINE, SO THE MAN THOUGHT HIS WIFE WAS GOING POTTY WHEN HE HEARD HER SAY, **'WATCH OUT FOR THE RAIN, DEAR.'** THEN A REINDEER LANDED ON HIS HEAD.

WHAT DO FAIRIES, PIXIES AND DWARVES RELY ON WHEN THEY ARE ILL?
THE NATIONAL ELF SERVICE.

All the kids had gathered at Sunday school, sitting on the floor around the teacher.
'NOW,' said the teacher, 'CAN ANYONE TELL ME WHY WE SHOULD ALWAYS BE QUIET IN THE CHURCH?'
'BECAUSE PEOPLE ARE SLEEPING, MISS,' said one little boy.

HOW DID THE BEACH GET ALL WET?
The sea weed.

TWO BISHOPS WERE ASLEEP IN BED. WHICH ONE WAS WEARING A NIGHTIE?
MRS BISHOP.

WHICH ITEM OF CLOTHING CAN DO 120 MPH?
HONDA PANTS.

A VICAR WAS IN COURT,
HAVING BEEN ARRESTED.
'WHAT ON EARTH ARE YOU DOING HERE,
VICAR?' ASKED THE JUDGE.
'I WAS RIDING MY BICYCLE THE WRONG
WAY UP A BUSY ONE-WAY STREET,'
SAID THE VICAR.
'WELL, I HAVE TO FINE YOU £25 FOR THAT,'
SAID THE JUDGE. 'WEREN'T YOU
FRIGHTENED IN ALL THAT TRAFFIC?'
'NO, THE LORD WAS WITH ME,'
SAID THE VICAR.
'IN THAT CASE I HAVE TO FINE
YOU ANOTHER £25 FOR HAVING TWO
ON A BIKE!'

What do you call a nun who goes sleep walking?

A ROAMIN' CATHOLIC.

Where is the creepiest place to go for a Sunday picnic?

LAKE EERIE.

What kind of snake would you use on your car windscreen.

A VIPER.

When you're out on a picnic, what's the best thing to do if you are allergic to biting insects?

Try not to bite any.

A vicar was asleep in the middle of the night when the doorbell rang. Both the vicar and his wife were woken by the persistent ringing and the vicar went downstairs to answer the door.

'CAN YOU GIVE ME A PUSH?' said the man standing on the doorstep. **'DON'T BE RIDICULOUS!'** snapped the vicar. **'IT'S THE MIDDLE OF THE NIGHT!'** And he slammed the door shut.

When he went back up to bed and

told his wife what had happened, she said:

'I know it's a nuisance, dear, but if our car had broken down, I'd like to think that someone would help us to get it started. Giving him a push would be the Christian thing to do, and you are a vicar.'

So the vicar went back downstairs, opened the front door and called out into the darkness: 'OKAY, I'LL GIVE YOU A PUSH. WHERE ARE YOU?'

'SITTING OVER HERE ON YOUR GARDEN SWING.'

The Sunday school was preparing
for Christmas.

'Now, who can tell me how many
reindeer pull Santa's sleigh?'
asked the teacher.

'Two,' answered Colin. 'Rudolph and Olive.'

'Rudolph is correct,' said the
teacher, 'but why did
you say Olive?'

**'Because it's in the
song,' said Colin.**

'Rudolph the red-nosed
reindeer, Had a very shiny
nose, And if you ever
saw it, You would even
say it glowed. Olive
the other reindeer . . .'